"As Steven Swank
and here in this collect.
purpose of a gentle and concentrated attentiveness. Traversing continents, experiences, and myriad questions, as well as diverse relationships with family, friends, strangers and creatures, this poetry captures the gaze of a peace-seeker looking within for solace and strength. A generous and compassionate poet, Swank extends to us the gift of his sportive voice in earnest verse, enfolding our attention."
—*Anupama Amaran, Writer, Editor, Educator*

"Steve's observations are stunning; they can be poignant, hilarious and heartbreaking. Always accessible and thought provoking, his poetry makes me want to slow down to be more observant of life around me."
—*Eric Weidman*

"Steven's poems are pure philosophy, day-to-day inspirations revealing the soul. A rhyme echoes a line of prose, interrupts, and yet does not, for each work is a whole, in Steven's dry, thoughtful voice, an invitation to mindfulness. You might think that a book of so many poems would become repetitious; it does not, as each poem touches a familiar scene, a different theme, an incident, a love, a goose, a town afraid of trees. It is life unfolded. One hundred and eighty pages, and yet I'd be glad for more."
—*Jeremy Salter,*
Co-author of
The 101 Most Influential People Who Never Lived.

"The best books of poems have great range. This is one of them. Steven Swank has chosen the perfect title for his new collection. It unfolds like an origami flower, revealing unexpected angles at every turn. His whimsy is blessedly intelligent, effortlessly meaningful. As Auden said of

Forster, he 'trips us up like an unnoticed stone' and coaxes us to chuckle with him at the breathtaking absurdities of life. But these witty, lighthearted songs are matched page for page by much deeper material that reflects an acute and reticent heart hoping each instant for connections to others. Join him, and your world will get brighter."

—*Barry Sheinkopf,*
author of What There Was *and* Collected Poems

UNFOLD

1 July 2017

DEAREST
DEB — ii

Thank you for ever
being my friend!

Steven Smith

See DEDICATION —
Page 36, 136, 182

ALSO BY STEVEN SWANK
The Horse Knows: Selected Poems

UNFOLD

Selected Poems, 2014–2016

STEVEN SWANK

Full Court Press
Englewood Cliffs, New Jersey

First Edition

Copyright © 2017 by Steven Swank

Published in the United States of America
by Full Court Press, 601 Palisade Avenue,
Englewood Cliffs, NJ 07632
fullcourtpressnj.com

ISBN 978-1-938812-91-0
Library of Congress Catalog No. 2017936864

For more information about the author visit his website:
creativeimperatives.com

Editing and book design by Barry Sheinkopf forBookshapers
(bookshapers.com)

Cover art by the author

The author gratefully acknowledges the prior appearance of
"Stone Head" in *River River*

To THOSE GIVING OF THEMSELVES

for the healing and benefit of others; those
working toward peace, justice, and
reconciliation; those working and living in
ways that support the well-being of creatures
great and small as we learn new harmonies
with the planet, I dedicate this book.

ACKNOWLEDGMENTS

I emphatically credit Daryl, Cara, Becca,
Zac, family, friends, and mentors Barry
Sheinkopf and Anupama Amaran, whose
love, patience, and encouragement
capacitate my expressive ventures.

TABLE OF CONTENTS

—2015—

A boat is safe in the harbor,
but this is not the purpose of a boat.

—Paulo Coelho

UNFOLD

I push *Command-N*
and a new blank page appears.
The screen is more opaque,
more illusionary,
than the screen on my door
that lets the fresh, dewy
air of morning fill the kitchen.

The sanitary blankness
waits the arrival of keystrokes,
waits thoughts in my head
to coalesce in some way meaningful,
leaping synapse to synapse,
linking syllable to syllable
to express purpose, passion,
like a recipe, a prayer.

I try to track the movements
as if a thousand chimps
are swinging
randomly through treetops
of their mountain home
before the early fog has lifted.
Though I feel the urge,
endeavor speech,
I see no pattern,
I discern no path.

Now, just now you appear,

bright in my unfocused memory
a point of light toward which
I turn in recognition, in hope,
ready to let the drama of day
unfold unencumbered, unafraid.

2014

A WORTHWHILE FIRE

We have started a worthwhile fire—
let tender flame kindle, ignite.

We cuddle and watch it aspire
to be consumed as heat and light.

As I Read It

As I read the poem, I know who wrote it,
I hear your voice in every line,
I see your smiling mouth articulate each sound.

Each stanza's fabric flows more graceful
because you place with care
and fill the shape with passion

I feel the vowels, peach and lavender,
tenderly caress the edgy consonants
that you so skillfully imbue.

Bird Splashes

Behind the house,
a tulip tree,
in the shade a basin;
this breezeless morning
a robin bathes.

And though an inch of water
is smallish depth,
the robin splashes joyously
and ruffles in delight
as if it is an ocean.

So it is, whenever
we chance to meet,
no matter how briefly,
my soul is refreshed
in waves of emotion.

BLACK LEATHER JACKET

Years later, as you clean out the closet
and I am working nearby,
you find his black leather jacket.

When he left finally,
he must have forgotten
it was still hanging on.

As neither he nor it
suited you or fit,
you give it to me.

If ever he and I cross paths,
I'm just one of a million guys
wearing a black leather jacket.

CLAPPER

Who has silenced our bell
that it does not ring?
Who has removed our clappers
that we do not sing?

Who has silenced the bell
that it does not ring?
Who has removed the clapper
that you do not sing?

CONNECTEDNESS

An oak leaf has settled on the grass and flutters
in sight and sound like wings of a bird.

The bird bath has barely thawed around the rim
but enough for a squirrel to delicately sip.

The tulip tree seeds dropped from branches
during fall are eaten by ravenous grackles.

Hardly thirty feet square, yet in a yard so small,
lying on the grass, a calm accrues to me.

Looking out the back door this morning
I am surprised to see a coyote in the early light.
With long hairs bright, golden, tan, white
enveloping its coat, in a dozen paces
she easily traverses our shared space,
pauses just long enough for me to notice,
then casually leaps the neighbor's fence, amused.

CRAZY DEAD PEOPLE

1,000 crazy dead people
buried long ago behind the asylum
have been found just where
the University of Mississippi
wanted to put the parking garage.

The engineers told the administrators
it would cost 3,000 dollars per grave
to move those crazy people,
the price three million dollars.
They therefore remain undisturbed.

Apparently the crazy dead
are not without voice enough
to express the wildness within them
now manifest in thriving greenery,
a path, a park, and trees.

Thanks to their chorus,
toddlers, children, lovers
will wander in innocence
among the oaks and cedars
above their unmarked graves.

CREWS ARE CUTTING

Crews
are cutting
down the trees
in our town now because
in recent years several storms have
caused tree-related damage. Ads by
companies wanting to make great sums
of money from the tree-trimming and removal
have flooded the community with promises,
free estimates, and easy payments. The propaganda
of fear and paranoia has eviscerated common sense.
Friends and neighbors have not been immune
from anxious contagion. The willingness of our
population to live with risk, or an amusing sense
that life is a chancy proposition, has all
but disappeared. One of the reasons
we moved here is for the small-town
feel and tree-lined streets.
Trucks with
booms, men,
tools, have
descended on
our town like
locusts. They
saw, hack, and
bundle living,
even thriving
members of our
community into
chippers, onto trucks.

CRYSTALS

Crystals grow naturally,
under pressure, in the void,
cooling volcanic spews.

Some crystals form
under crushing weight
over eons of time.

Others, like amusement
in a child's fish bowl,
grow in colored hues.

Poems react to pressures;
they bend, compress, falter,
accumulating rhyme.

Dear Heart

The weight or mass
of our perceptions, expectations,
warps the reality through which we move.

As a star warps space,
you move me.

DINNER IN MOONLIGHT

The village chief of Segou, Senegal,
invites us to dine with his family.

We eat dinner in moonlight
outside their tribal hut.

We are their guests because they host my son
as a Peace Corps volunteer.

My son converses in Pular and French,
consulting and laughing with ease.

Clearly they treat him affectionately,
say they're honored to meet his father.

I am proud of my son and glad for this opportunity
to see him engaging with the world.

They share their common bowl of onion rice
with *toubabs* from America.

As we converse, they notice how slow I eat
and ask about my appetite.

I say I am too hot to eat,
and ask them to consume my portion.

Their hands reach out across the bowl,
removing every kernel.

ÉTREINTE

She knows:
the science of tender embrace
how to caress a dream
charm vipers
keeps wolves at bay
remove lint from a collar
prepare a meal without harm
hug a stranger
hostess a party
or if you make her cross,
how to bar the door.

FOREVER MY LOVE

If you go away, I will remember you;
if you lose the way back to me,
still I hold you.
In my mind you are never out of sight,
never far from me;
my heart is wrapped around yours.

If I wander in my thoughts, hold me close,
know my caring self endures,
you are, ever, my love.

GLACIAL AQUIFER

The glacially fed, contained aquifer,
being sucked for corporate gain,
will not be refreshed in many lifetimes—
yet we permit the pump, the drain.

HEY, POPS!
(by Zac Swank, 2014)

We were remiss in the purchase of Father's Day cards,
so I thought I would send an e-poem-ish thingy.

He's now my friend
but still chases monsters away

He doesn't have all the answers
but still answers my questions.

He helps me figure it all out
while he still figures it out.

He is vulnerable and open and strong
and brave and the kind of dad
who rescues his babies from apple trees.

He's you. My dad. And I love him.

STEVEN SWANK

HONK, HONK

I congratulate myself
for being early
as I walk toward
the dentist's office.

Traversing the parking lot
I hear *honk, honk*
and, jumping aside, I look
but see no car approaching.

I walk several more paces
again I hear, honk, honk.
Turning, I am startled to see
a Canada goose glide
through the space
where I was just standing
its wingtip nearly brushing
my shoulder. It lands
just beyond my shadow.

The poem
in real time
takes four seconds.

I am here,
I hear *honk,*
I turn, and the goose
is here also.

If When You Rise

If, when you rise, you find my note,
hear the beat my heart is drumming.

If, when you rise, the day is dim,
the lamp you light gets me humming.

I HEAR YOU WEEPING

Mother,
I hear you weeping far away for your son
in another country, in another tongue.
I hear you weeping,
I hear you weeping,
I hear you weeping.
I expect you are busy doing what needs,
figuring out what can be done.
I send creative energy to you,
peace of spirit to strengthen your heart.
Please remember to eat and breathe.
I hold you in heart, mind, body, soul.

Love,
Steve

KITCHEN DOOR

As he hangs the kitchen door,
my son explains that termites
are a problem relentless as the tide
here in his West African village.

The door is made of corrugated
metal roofing over a wood frame.
The hinges, imbedded into the mud wall,
he attaches to the wood frame with screws.

The kitchen is three meters square.
It stands separate
from the thatched pavilion roof
that will be the dining area
in the eco-tourist lodge
he is facilitating.

Within a week the termites have begun
to make covered mud tunnels
across the walls to the door opening
and onto the hinges so they have access
to the swinging wood frame.

As a Toubab soon returning home,
it amuses that I think to alter Africa
on my last day by once more wiping off
the tubular trails of termites.

MARGARITA

Critique what you will
or like what you must,
when you come for lunch
and I, coming from the barn,
appear rumpled and dusty,
forgive me the hayseed
in my hair when we embrace.

We will defer to the kittens
asleep on the porch chairs,
walk our meal to the bridge.
As we sit we will watch the water,
hear the birds, engage the babble.

MEDITATIONS WITH CATS

A truck pulls in the drive.
A man gets out and shouts me awake,
asking why I am lying in the yard.
I reply, I nap with cats to meditate.

If I settle to nap mid-afternoon,
they find me on the dappled grass
and, unconcerned, leap on my still form
or bite my toes.

Another day, as the rain drips
from trees and roof, the kittens
curl up beside momma and me
asleep on the welcome mat.

Or we might be found sitting
early on the side porch
watching the sun rise
through the trees.

We find comfort being
matched in breath as her kittens,
so rambunctious,
chase and tumble.

OMISSION

The book I am reading has a velvet cover,
is a heft to hold, its pages edged with gold.

Titled *The Anthology of Modern Poetry*,
yet it contains no poems by or about you.

William Cullen Bryant in his introduction
does not mention or reflect on the omission.

Your name does not appear as a byline or in any
of the many footnotes, but there you are,

in the tragedy, in the praise, in the tears of exhalation,
or the crushing weight of neglectful indifference.

Despite being overlooked, I see you looking out at me.
You are found in the wit, envy, pathos, humor.

Had I not found you it would be as if
the periodic table contained no oxygen.

POEMS FROM THE PICKLE JAR

I plucked words from the vine,
put them in jars of pickle brine,
placed the lot on basement shelves,
in a couple months came back to find
if the words arranged themselves
into the poems I had in mind.

I must admit a few looked sad,
but they weren't the worst I ever had.
None were moldy, puce, or brown,
though some had flipped to upside-down.

Among the jars, there were a couple
that were good and lean and supple.
Some that had snap were crisp with crunch;
when you visit, I'll serve with lunch.

POLITICS OF THE NEW

The joy of something new, how quickly it passes—
like the politician once was of the masses.

Mornings I do proportional math—
why won't the water drain from my bath?

RED FLAGS

Red flags with black squares
flap in unison from the harbor pole
as the storm approaches,
the surge and tide scour beaches,
inundate homes and reaches
where silly man will forget
and build again.

Because we forget in such short a while
do I cry or, knowing, smile?

ROAD TRIP

I am away when you visit;
a neighbor's car is in our driveway.

You ring the bell, knock on the door,
look in the window. The porch has chairs.

Driving home another six hours
is a lot of time for you to wonder

Are old friends worth the effort,
risk-averse, troubling disappointments?

You care enough to see what happens,
and update me with a phone call.

ROWING TOGETHER

As I was out on the water rowing,
you noticed me
struggling against the wind,
offered to man one oar.

I am writing to thank you,
not only for your labor,
but also especially
for your joyous companionship.

SEE SOMETHING, SAY

We often see something,
but are unsure when, if,
we should say something.

I see great disparity
in this country:
Should I say something?

I see first hand
the science of climate change:
Should I say something?

I see our nation
turning into an oligarchy:
Should I say something?

I hear false statements
made on the radio:
Should I say something?

I see falsehoods on TV
portrayed as fact:
Should I say something?

Should we say something?
We should say something!
We should *do* something!

STILL THE GUYS

The village folk are hunkered down,
the temp is 4, and chilled by winds
toward 22 below.
Unlike Buffalo, getting
three feet of snow,
we have none.

Still, the trash pickup guys,
usually jovial in conversation,
yell, Go.
Go.
Go!

THE GNAT

The gnat we treat
with such disdain,
its life we think so small—
and yet,
intelligence that it displays
may be greater far
than all the life on Mars.

THE MAN WHO READS

The man who reads books
is homeless and sleeps
tucked in the void
of a construction site fence.

Each day she walks by
on her way to work
and sees him there
in his half-box house.

As he slumbers,
the two-toned pooch
curled beside him
raises its head.

The dog and she
acknowledge with looks
both kind and sympathetic,
though neither speaks.

When he is gone
the radio and books
hold his place like marking a page
so no one's inclined to disturb his spot.

She sees that he reads
cultured fare: Shakespeare,
Glinka, Hemingway,
Grimes, Voltaire.

He reads about the Arctic,
life on the moon, indigenous cultures,
philosopher kings,
the politics of nations, astrophysical things.

And books telling how to do the stuff
she wishes she knew: plumbing, weaving,
scrimshaw, how to make perfect
mashed potatoes.

She cannot imagine a life
so free and yet so hard
as she leaves him the gift
of a library card.

THE MOBILE

My balance is steady in equilibrium
through the distribution of force and mass,
weights and levers, fulcrum, pendulums,
that earns me An Artist plaque in brass.

I start with a bag of saddest sand
suspended by cables and ironic means
salvaged from the scrap heaps
and wastes of industrial scenes.

There also hang doubts aplenty
on branches impossibly thin,
bending just shy of breaking,
that one day will do me in.

How's it possible you wonder,
to counter that weight drawn under
with such slender dreams and hopes
against the odds, among the nopes.

Like the balance, skipping stones on the pond,
countervailing forces, I respond.
Every day the sadness has been in my life;
every day I feel the draw of its knife.

I balance with counterweights and pleasure.
How long the levers need be, I can measure,
attaching humor to thousands of strings
that fly like kites, dispiriting things,

into the winds of adventure, thus keeping
the disturbing darkness from my sleeping.

The joy is in self, meditation, sweat,
as I work with my hands, the closer I get
to being well-balanced on both my feet
and ready to greet you whenever we meet.

Your love and friendship are among
the reasons my song can be sung;
it stretches sweetly in an arch, bending
just enough to keep me fending.

Always I'm conscious, always knowing
where is the tipping, and is it showing.

THE PROVIDENCE OF YOUR SMILE

There is magic, I am convinced:
I see it in the generosity,
the providence of your smile

the way your mouth forms
like a child in glee. Without
a word, it lights your eyes.

The warmth of your being
fills my waiting heart
though my train departs.

Will you be there when I return
is the question that's in doubt;
I love you! I turn and shout.

TODAY I DUSTED

Cara, today I dusted
the little picture frame,
the three of you smiling
into the camera lens.

You were young, I was home,
we were happy.

TONIGHT

Tonight I am eating
for the first time
at this diner.

My expectations
are not very high.
I am not disappointed.

The waitress asks me
to tip her in cash or
the cashier steals it.

I get cake to go,
finish the water,
pocket crackers.

In the parking lot
a broken pencil; the
wind is damp and raw;

inside a parked car,
a slouching woman cradles
her head in darkness.

UPDRAFT

The clouds look so unusual,
I drive two miles up the escarpment;
from the promontory overlook
I can see thirty miles.

Now nearly at eye level
with the forming storm,
I watch in fascination as it grows
and gathers momentum.

Building rapidly, the breeze
turns to come from behind
as it is pulled into the updraft,
and strong!

I lift my collar against the chill.
The darkening mass begins to rotate,
then pitches gray wisps
downward in slow motion.

I have the urge to duck
as it passes overhead,
and later learn the tornado
touched down five miles away.

VERMONTERS

Vermonters are humble,
we most never boast,
but our products make
the most of your toast.

WHAT IS THAT SOUND?

What is that sound I wonder as I wake.
Is someone on the roof using a rake?

It is too raspy and loud to be the refrigerator;
a low-flying plane I think it is not.

Perhaps a snowplow blade is scraping,
the crew inside all high on pot.

The windows shudder, the panes all rattle
like the thundering hooves of panicking cattle.

Is a neighbor at my door, pounding with his fist?
Ah—it's my wife's pencil; she's making my list.

WHEN

When she's hot, she takes off some clothes.
As I turn the heat up, do you think she knows?

WHEN WE KISS

When we kiss, you are
too busy to notice.
You are living in the future,
I am living in the past.

I walk a couple of blocks
out of my way just to watch
the municipal guys remove snow
from the parking lot.

A front loader scoops
the ashen snow banks,
dumping them into trucks
while cars wait to park.

I say goodbye to the snow;
it looks tired and worn out
as if its energy and life
have vanished or expired.

As the hearse drives by, I wave,
but you do not wave back.
Perhaps you do not see me
from inside the dark casket.

How fast the light, giddy days
of our expressive passions
settle and drift into routine,
succumb to indifference.

We are too soon melted,
too soon carted away;
may we again be united
in the flow of a great river.

Women with Tattoos

It is not for amusement, if that's what you think,
that causes some women to acquire the ink—
they won't brag about the marks
drawn on their chests,
put there by technicians who irradiate breasts.

You Can't See the Forest

You cannot see the forest
because there are no trees.

2015

ADVERSITY

Adversity and obstacles obstruct the flow
and thus become a pause,
affording us a newer grasp to show
how we might now more rightly have our say.

They interrupt, show how we've grown
and cause us in midstream
to leap from stone to stone,
to get new ideas and find a better way.

A Worthwhile Fire II

How will I keep warm now that you are gone?

I wake early and wonder, what will I burn today—
the searing memories of our relationship,
the scar tissue of our last conversation
in November rain at the graveyard?

During the gray-dawn months of winter
I set to blaze a worthwhile fire,
create a vacancy enough each day for insight,
a warmth of heart that stretches round the hearth.

In the furnace of desire, let burn
the angst and debris, to be warm at last.

Back to the Mine

My grandfather left the mine
to work the steel plant.
My father left the steel plant
to work the farm.

I have worked the steel plant,
worked the farm,
and now I work the mine
with modest tools, my lamp
burning in the dark.

I look for you,
find only tracks.

The gems of iron sulfide,
onyx, jade,
are glittering distractions
but hold no warmth,
express no joy.

I look for you.

BRICOLAGE

bricolage |☒brēkō☒lä zh; ☒brik☒-|
noun (pl. same or **-lages**)
(in art or literature) construction or creation from a diverse range of available things : *the chaotic bricolage of the novel is brought together in a unifying gesture.*
• something constructed or created in this way : *bricolages of painted junk.*
ORIGIN mid 20th cent.: French, from **bricoler 'do odd jobs, repair.'**

Can we together
find the means to build
with available bricks?

With bricks for ballast
we will manage
to do with balance.

CHILDREN LATE FOR SCHOOL

Dear teacher,
Please excuse my children—
they are late for school.

We were up late last night
on the roof watching the stars;
they were brilliant—did you see?

We went at dawn to watch
circus elephants set up tents,
and only now have returned.

On our walk to school,
beavers were building.
We stopped to watch.

Children helped deliver calves today,
came then to school. Do they smell?
Please excuse.

Will pick up children at noon—
are traveling to Washington, DC,
to see how government works.

We are driving across the country,
will be gone nine weeks.
Have books, don't worry.

Crows

Crows are on the spring house
(the roof long gone),
sit atop rafters while it rains
and face into the wind
like weather vanes.

They hum and caw
to announce their morning watch
has begun, and as I pass
they turn—one, then one,
then one.

Cycles

The price per hundred, the cost per pound,
who makes the coffee, how many scoops;
were the keys lost, where were they found,
who jumps high, who holds the hoops?

Moments cycle like days,
heart beats per minute, hours, years,
the number of times I don't call you
because my eyes are full of tears.

DEAR CHILD

I will protect you from harm or hurt
as best I'm able.

I will love you though you must
push me away.

My notions for you may not fit or be
what you choose.

We will endure if we embrace
our differences.

EARLY

1.

We have arrived too early—
this poem is still sleeping.

2.

I was not ready,
I was not prepared,
to meet you so early.

Maybe later I would have spoken,
chanced the conversation,
and we could be friends.

Finally I am ready,
I am prepared;
where are you?

Fellow Writers

I miss you all when I am not at Write;
busy with drama, work,
the press of necessity,
the frightful abyss.

FOUR

Four cops
take down the homeless man
in a convenience store aisle
while his daughter yells,
"Daddy, Daddy!"

They choke him to death,
doing their duty, they claim.
What is their race,
what is his color?

What forces push them
to murder this man?
In what cup do we measure
serve and protect?

Five

I spill five grains of rice on the floor,
sweep them up, then toss to trash.
A mother somewhere covets them
to feed her crying child fussing with hunger.

The energy I burn driving five blocks
for groceries or incidentals
would fuel her stove for the day
over which she huddles
for warmth and cooking.

Five is the number of gallons of water
I use in a couple of casual flushes.
It is the amount in the bucket,
carried from the well on someone's head,
allotted each day to my son who sleeps
in a hut while working in Africa.

HOLDING ON

You said you are on hold,
so I wonder onto what
are you holding?

I picture you holding onto:

       a plank in the ocean,
       a skunk in the hall,
       a mirror on the subway,
       a breath in the movie,
       a bell at the park,
       a tightrope between buildings,
       a sandwich in the dark,
       a teaspoon of applesauce,
       a fire hose,
       a vine swinging over the creek,
       a high-flying goose,
       a large thrashing fish,
       a moonbeam over ice,
       a hatching chick,
       an open umbrella,
       the sound of rabbits.

I HAVE

I have been thinking about you.
   Where are you?

I have a pen that works.
   Where are you?

I have time to share.
   Where are you?

I have creative license.
   Where are you?

I have E-Z Pass.
   Where are you?

I have great resilience.
   Where are you?

I have questions and potential.
   Where are you?

I have not given up.
   Where are you?

I have a good sense of direction.
   Where are you?

I have returned your refrigerator.
   Where are you?

I have looked for you in Tuscany.
    Where are you?

I have brought you flutes from Peru.
    Where are you?

I have learned the flambé.
    Where are you?

I have an enduring love.
    Where are you?

Have I said too much?

IF I

If I were sick, you might visit,
but if I'm well,
you never do. Why so is it?

When you are sick, I bring you soup,
or if you're well,
I'm on your stoop waiting to be noticed.

Why do you never stop by or call?
We could chat, or we might
find awkward things to untie.

Still, you would so be nice to see,
your voice to hear,
embrace, and hold.

INADVERTANTISM

Def. 1; The functioning belief that life is chancy; as a group these practitioners are known as Inadvertantists.

Def. 2; A small sect of the faith Not For Rhyme Or Reason, who espouse that all events are happenstancical. It is thought probable that this group first stickerized their bumpers with the legend *Shit Happens For A Reason, Or Not.*

LAUNDRY

The leaf hops like a toad,
sideways then forward
through the underbrush,
through my mind,
whimsy in errant breezes.

Women at river edge
wash clothes, beat on rocks,
wring by hand, hang on bushes
in the sun to dry,
as cattle roam nearby.
Mothers keep watchful eyes
on the children and crocodiles.

Here on this continent
we launder by machine,
evolve the clothespin
to be spring loaded.

LORENA

My grandfather Horace would walk eight miles
up into the hills to visit his child Lorena
while she convalesced in the TB sanatorium.

He brought her food from home,
and some days he carried a shotgun
to hunt rabbits on the way.
Upon his arrival a nurse would place
the gun and rabbits out of view.

Lorena recovered but felt thereafter at risk
and did not participate in the adventures
and meanders of her brothers and cousins.
At the end of her life, paralyzed from a stroke,
she refused food or drink and, thus determined,
chose to chance what happens next.

I wonder, would I be that brave?

Mandala

Arching forward
above the mandala
with care and balance,
his outstretched arms
suspend slender fingers
that drizzle colored sand
as the intricate disk emerges.

Beside him,
squatting angels
observe, and slowly
flex their wings.

Traveling Shoes
(for Steve, by Marcy Telles)

Your traveling shoes are ready,
you best be on your way
my kisses are an echo,
and we know you cannot stay.

Oh, your eyes are looking restless
when they look deep into mine;
you hold me very tightly now,
to make me friends with time.

But the eagle has to fly in the sun;
soon you're gone.

Funny about changes—
when you try to look away
they build up all around you,
in some crystal-patterned way.

Oh, I know I live in cages,
but I've learned to travel slow;
I see their fingers on you,
and I see you wistful go,

and I reach my hand out in goodbye—
perhaps I sigh.

Love is like some ocean,

both here and beyond,
and we are only islands
in the ocean's gentle wash.

I know about the distance,
and that's why I said good-bye,
but our love is not in inches,
and I guess we'll bide with time,

and the eagle leaves his nest for sun;
soon you're gone, darling—travel on.

Marcy,

I am so sorry, and saddened to hear this news. I had no idea you have headed toward the next room. I love you so much! You are a star shining bright in my universe. You have shown me much love, compassion, and tenderness in our long friendship. From the beginning you have changed my life, through love, humor, and honesty. I adore and thank you for that.

Always always,
Steve

HOW LOVELY

How lovely and grand—
like a fine grain of sand
or single hair strand
I find in the comb.
You are home.

I FAINT FROM DISTANCE

Time and space cannot create this much distance;
only hearts apart can do that.

Sometimes dreams change;
sometimes it is the dreamers who change.

Sometimes it takes a lifetime.

I JUST

I just read your little note,
am touched by what you wrote.
Crumbs are small comfort.

Dear Friend,
I miss you also,
and there in the missing—
a comfort,
to have you as friend.

With great affection,
Steve

REFUGEES

We smell of earth and hunger, want—
our voices silent, our eyes are not.

ROW

While we sort for a better idea,
we row with the oars we have.

STEVEN SWANK

SHOULD I

Should I admit the ability to swerve
off the beaten path, away from convention?

How suddenly routine and schedule
are jettisoned to follow
the novel, capricious thought
of a poem on the horizon,
the mast of which is just visible
beyond the arc of consciousness.

Small Books

1.

'Twas in small books
I learned to read,
see and walk with Jane.
The stories then
were very plain.

Later small books
explained the assembly,
what size pots for cooks,
guides to foreign lands
if travel was in my plans.

But still the book
I most wish to know
is about kindness,
love and strength,
what we get to show.

2.

The book is small
page to page,
words with space

try each day
expressing life,

the content, joy.

I've been away,
abated death,
returned home

but you're gone.
Still, we danced,
stepped in time.

3.

You are a treasure,
do you see it?
Beat and measure
like the Sanskrit

The smallest book
or largest cup,
you have the will
to fill it up.

Across the table,
meditating,
calm and breath,
we are able.

Poetry is gleaning
in the borderlands,
the margins,
words and meaning.

THE CHAIR

Until you sit in it,
the chair is only potential,
its purpose unrealized,
as if no water burst forth
from the fountains of Rome.

When you settle there,
it vibrates with life;
Villa Giulia, Triton, Villa Medici, and Trevi
alive in Respighi's sweep of strings,
oboes, brass, delicate bells.

THE DAY

The day clanged shut
with all the mechanical heft
of an industrial overhead door,
its motorized throbbing sprockets
engaged, unrelenting.

I hope soon
to see you,
to see the sun.

THE EDGE

I live on the edge of your space, your language,
in the borderland of night that is not yet,
though the sun is mostly set.

I look for you among the silhouettes,
your presence among the shadows.

If we ever find a way together in some fashion,
a common place or time, let us begin again,
express the rhyme of passion.

Let us find mutual capacities for speech
to touch—finally freed from the past, see how
we might celebrate the now.

STEVEN SWANK

THEY DID NOT, BUT STILL

They did not marry after all,
but still they love each other
though they seldom write
and mostly never call.

They both have children
fully grown, moved away,
living on their own,
living in foreign lands.

The daughter, Sam,
teaches in Madrid,
the son, in The Peace Corps,
lives in Africa. It's hot.

He misses hearing her breathe,
the sound of her voice—
wonders, when they said goodbye,
was it a necessary choice?

WHAT LUCK

We just might be the happiest people
we meet all day. What luck for us.
We have the intelligence to observe all that,
and also know that we have the capacity
to determine how we feel about what we see.
Are we gaining or losing? We do the choosing.

What She Says

Don't go to bed too early,
don't get up too late,
please sit up straight
as much as you are able,
please clear your plate
as you leave the table.

WHOSE FOOT

Whose
foot
is
the
other
shoe
on?

WHEN WE

When we arrived too early for that other poem,
did you wait for me?

WINDMILLS

There are windmills! Pick up our lances,
get on our horses, and take some chances.

Get to starting, and, as we go,
we'll learn the things to know.

In My Mind

You are in my mind
like moonlight on the lake
at summer's end.

You are in my mind
abruptly like leaps
of the fox.

You are in my mind
like sharp foot pain
at the ballet.

You are in my mind
like the howling yips
coyote makes in rain.

You are in my mind
like performance anxiety
opening night.

You are in my mind
like the buzz
of an attic fly.

You are in my mind
like a cat's twitching
anticipation.

You are in my mind
like a welcoming campfire
at dusk.

You are in my mind
like the delight
of a child's laugh.

You are in my mind
like early budding, promise
of spring.

You are in my mind
like the taste of berries
on the tongue.

You are in my mind
like long shadows
on snow.

YOU SHINE

How lovely to know your tenderness
in the dark of my night.
You shine brightest among the stars.

Your smiles from summer
I have stacked like firewood,
kept sheltered from the rain.

During frightful winter storms
I burn them in my hearth
to keep me warm and happy.

ZAC

You were not the doctor with the knife,
but you knew enough to save her life;
when she saw not the urgency,
you took her to Emergency.

If we tune our time and place,
opportunities find us.

2016

STEVE SWANK

ANU

Thank you for our writing group.
Each of us bring our own story,
imagination, choice.

All in tender mercy speak
in humble words our fancy;
each finds here a voice.

ALLIGATOR

It did not seem that dangerous at first—
I just wanted to pet its head.
What could happen, at best, at worst?
I thought that it was slumbering,
it looked so calm, or was it dead?
Danger is all the sign had said.

I was off the path, I admit.
Really, it could happen to anyone.
I did not think I'd get bit,
the gator was just a little one.
Because blood makes me nauseous,
my friends said, I should be cautious.

Yet my momentum went unabated.
Reaching toward the reptile,
my whole face began to smile.
Look out! they shouted as I waded.
So quick I turned, and leapt about
just as Momma snapped her snout.

Her teeth caught hold of my laces,
her twist and lurch tore off my shoe,
I scampered up the muddy bank.
Then we watched with startled faces
to see what next thing it would do,
the baby climbed onto her scaly flank.

When they emerged on the other shore,
we noticed what was there:
a bunch, a pile, a profoundish mound
of every imaginable kind of footwear!
Now there too, mine could be found
as she dropped it on the ground.

With binoculars I could clearly see
boots, clogs, sneakers, flip-flops, loafers,
polished shoes once worn by chauffeurs,
and fisherman waders by a tree.
Careful viewing also reveals
a vast array of high heels.

After that, we had to laugh—
for all the danger and commotion
the gators had their own promotion.
Since they reduced my pair by half,
they'd release the shoe, for a fee,
a scrawlish sign stated plainly:

Lose your shoe in all that the muck?
Buy it back for just a buck.
A brisk business's being had.
Our retail staff is just too glad
to help you find yours in the pile.
The line is long—it takes a while.

I am convinced—well, pretty sure—
the little gator was just a lure,

a ploy, a pretense, ruse,
conniving way for snatching shoes.
The locals, I am told, obey the sign.
I won't give in, nor will I whine.

Grateful to escape with only scratches
I left my shoe to their scheming
and gimp without it every day.
Now each step has some meaning,
I pay attention to what signs say,
and no longer play with matches.

Alternate Paths

Today I walked the alternate path—
not the driveway so conveniently placed,
but rather 'round the house another way,
where the stone and brick walk,
in awkward, uneven dissymmetry,
imply hazard.

The choice to travel thus
created opportunity to notice,
be interactive with that side of life.
I plucked leaves from the bird bath,
engaged with smiling snow drops,
watched mice doing early forays.

ANOMIE

Helping a friend sail from Nyack to Norfolk,
we navigate long hours of ocean voyage
in late October chill,
seldom seeing another vessel.

Sailing in bright sun
and star-lit nights on uneven seas,
a calm envelops me;
though tired and cold, a wholeness
enthuses our companionship.

In harbor we meet other sailors,
both men and women,
who speak foreign tongues
yet soon become community.

I return by train,
then subway jammed with people
looking down at their phones;
here, I feel most awkward, alone.

ARBITRARIOSITY

The robin with a worm
dangling from its mouth
continues to hunt and peck
about the yard.

What I decide is
good for the robin
is not so good
for the worm.

How susceptible,
even capricious
are values, traditions,
choices.

ART AS PROTEST

1.

I am subverted by your smile,
the very idea of you.

As I breathe, so must I write,
the nature of which is risk
of censure from my culture, time.
The risk of art expressing
truth and insight that challenges
convention has always been dangerous.

Equally dangerous, perhaps more insidious,
is self-censorship,
the building of internal structures
that prevent light getting in
or our truth getting out—
a life of misery, starvation, sleepless calamity.

2.

I am subverted by your smile,
the very idea of you.

Each breath is a creative imperative,
the risk (as every artist knows) existential.

Censorship, whether applied

by external forces or internal ones,
has similar effects.

Artists, writers, poets
suffer equally the fate
of other free thinkers.

AS AN ARTIST

He mentioned, if it was up to him,
he would kill all the weeds.

As an artist, I was startled;
his comment made me nervous.

BATHE

Birds
basin
bathing

feathers
flap
flutter

water
wavers
wets

beaks
backs
butts

tails
twist
tremble.

BEDAZZLEMENT AND FRACTURE

You are the woman
who keeps us prompt—
watcher of the clock
who waits expectantly,
writes tiny script
in great detail
in small books,
exquisitely precise,

like the stars,
ever-present
steadfast

shining
unfathomable
light.

BUT ARE THEY WET?

Waves to shore
roll placid laps
in untormented calm,
like stripes on a cat
asleep in the window.

Waves to shore
break in gentle whispers,
under a half moon
like music memories
awake in a dream.

Waves to shore
though the depths are dark,
still twinkle with light
like stars of heaven's
sparkling children.

Waves to shore
progress in descent,
bid us enter
like fresh porch paint
on the farmhouse steps.

BUZZ

Do you know the buzz
of morning bees
come to visit blossoms
as early light catches
wings in motion?

If you wait for them
on the back step
in quiet stillness,
they will find you
to express gratitude
that you did not mow
the dandelions they nectar.

CLOTHES

These clothes I wear
protect you from my nakedness,
protect me from my own nakedness.

These clothes create the illusion
I fit in as part of the social norm,
capable of holding place.

DEAD END

The sign says *Dead End*;
still, it is the street
on which we live,
the trees grow,
and flowers blossom.

We have our lives,
no one dictates us,
we gather as friends
in joy or sorrow.

I like the community.
Among friends, feelings are safe;
we have lives of honesty.

With our backs to the wall,
the sun no longer shining,
a storm of police.

DEAR FRIEND

Greetings and well wishes,
the long days of summer,
peace and activity.

This week has been
busy at the opera,
making tables and more.

My evening's meditation
was moving stones
in the creek bed.

I watched salamanders,
toads, and spiders,
each unique and wonderful.

As I stood still there,
a Baltimore oriole
landed near to say hello.

I saw there too
humming birds
in courtship display.

Six varied bird songs
resounding off the barn
filled me with joy.

DEPTH AND BUOYANCY

We enter water,
marvel at buoyancy,
un-marveled perhaps,
the great depth sustaining us.

Some days,
though the water is shallow,
hardly ankle deep,
we feel we might drown.

DINER, FEBRUARY, RAIN

The man exits,
collar drawn up,
scarf around face,
hat pitched forward,
sunglasses on,
into rain.

Hostess speaks Russian,
seats her family,
kisses her mom,
counts tips,
orders food.
Her brother teases.

Old men talk across the aisle
in passionate tones,
discuss presidents dead,
movie actors past,
baseball players gone,
argue who'll pay the bill.

Late afternoon
at empty counter,
wait staff congregate,
backs to the register,
begin to vacuum;
kitchen crew emerges.

As the only customer left
I feel self-conscious,
Edward Hopperesque.
After paying my bill,
the dark lot empty,
I walk into the rain.

DISCIPLINE THE BLUSH

Enter through the gate,
discipline the blush,
build relationships with brick.

Tend the tender shoots,
bless them with light and laughter.
Let the ripples of your joy,
the bright of day,
radiate through community,
speak from the heart,
engage opportunity.

DO YOU

It is embarrassing to ask, so I never do,
still, do you love me? I wonder if you
think about me ever in that way.

If I never asked, would you say,
as if it'd just occurred, like an insight
(if I were leaning in, you might).

Would you blurt it out too loud
or state it nervously in a crowd,
or let it slip from your lips?

Because it's not like you at all,
if you wrote it on the wall,
would I question what I saw?

EARTH DAY 2016

Delicate blossoms drip with dew,
Tectonic plates subside,
Earth worms quietly renew,
Exploding stars send dust,
Half our cells are foreign microbes,
Gravitational waves ripple wells.

Nature's infinite wisdom
circulates pollen with flights of bees,
colonies of cooperative beings
organized for the common good,
benefiting plants and animals alike.

The Mekong Delta two foot above the sea
        produces one-fifth of our food.
Melting ice hungers bears, thawing permafrost,
        releases methane, raising sea level.

Corporations with no moral compass
        poison the bees for singular crop profits,
promote robotic flying insects, charging fees
        to service crop production.

Pollination no longer done by bees,
        where will we find the honey?

Though I have not your advantage,
I recognize the edge of a knife

You are not my enemy
yet threaten my life.

ENTER THROUGH THE GATE

1.

Portal, arch, gate on the horizon
wait for us patiently, silently,
unencumbered by dreams
or apprehension.

Progress in fits and spats,
delusion, happenstance;
we progress despite ourselves
in slow comprehension.

2.

Enter through the gate
read the sign;
having climbed over the fence,
dusted myself off,
I could now clearly see it.

Sipping peppermint tea
that is too hot to swallow,
I watch the tribe of scribes
write hurriedly in silence
while eating midday meals.

Declare yourselves, announce;
when we gather be true,

let be known your names
and where you imagine
the tongue must wander.

Ginger toasts,
salad gardeners,
psychic sandwiches,
rubenishes, omelettas,
keep our molars in motion.

All eyes look down,
intent, tasking fingers to write;
prompted feelings pour
into scrawling ventures
forcing time invents.

FOREST MIDDAY CHILD

During the night
follow your child
climb out the window

through the forest
sculpted moonlight
scented pine and salt.

Should the child tire
scoop them in arms
walk in blessedness

hush of conversation
quietly both assured
each let go concerns

find a spot of comfort
settle there to sleep
awake midday in ferns.

FORTUNE

A small baby bird lies dead in the driveway,
its limp feathers just beginning to show.

Squatting down, I observe
tiny ants working the small form.
Quickly my sadness
evolves to empathy
for the ants' good luck.
Kneeling nearby, I start weeding.

The call of a jay turns my attention—
looking over at the lifeless form,
I startle to see the blue jay land,
pluck it up swiftly, ants and all,
then fly away.
Stillness, calm. I am changed.

How quickly is fortune lost or found.

FRIEND

In a foreign city
on a distant continent
speaking a distant tongue
residing among strangers

living the compulsion
of creative passion—
endeavor your best;
park in a friendly space.

Be strong enough to matter—
the way forward
will not always be plain;
feed your soul, resolve.

Suffer the growth
you demand of self,
walk in the rain,
be warm at home.

With *bricolage* balance
work and family,
let joy be your doing,
love spill into place.

GRANDMA O.

Grand placement,
the things displayed
high on the shelf,
protected yet dusty—
the honored guests.

A pitcher and basin,
presents my grandmother
brought with her in 1906
through the port of New York
and Ellis Island.

She came from Smålund,
stony farm country
in the south of Sweden.
Aged sixteen, she asked,
if she might move to Stockholm.

A seamstress she would be.
Her mother said,
no, the city was too dangerous.
Grandma then asked,
could she go to America?

"America?
Yes, that would be okay,
your brothers are there."
"Then, I will go there," Grandma said,
and she did.

GROCERIES

Those are inside thoughts, she chastised me
as we walked in the grocery.

Honey, I say while pushing the cart,
in museums they show and call it art.

Not now, she adds, passing the jam,
each in our own way declaring, *I am.*

HARDLY KNOWING

I see you on the street sometimes;
if we converse, your pleasant smile
remains with me.

Can I call you friend?
I hardly know what to say
when we chance to meet.

Might we share ideas, joy?
Might we share a life concern
and thus extend our trust?

When I see you working
or in the public sphere,
I admire how you act,
your calm endorsement of others.

HIS THOUGHTS

His thoughts in the third person,
he sweats in awkwardness,
chances to have his say.

Scars of the heart shadow his path,
council harps encourage his steps,
angels unseen illuminate the way.

HOPE

I start this poem as I do each day,
hope by the end something gets said.

Writer, trouble the politics,
wander out the maze,
ponder past the obvious,
turn a truthful phrase.

HURRICANE

Stand in the center if that's your wont,
type if you must in the tinymost font,
grab your pajamas to sleep in the rain,
express your worries, just don't complain.

If storms clouds gather, you certainly might
have trouble sleeping sometimes at night,
the lightning and thunder inside your brain
like turbulent voices in howling disdain.

Pick up some crayons, go to the hall,
draw your fears all over the wall,
let go of troubles like kites on a string,
exhale the past. Jump. Shout. Sing.

I See

In the dark, up beyond the attic stairs,
past the geranium in the east window,
its silhouette backlit by the moon,
I see your eyes.

I Think Sometimes

I think sometimes
we wrestle with ourselves,
as if lovingly among angels.

It is to our credit
to also have friends
that behave this way.

JUJITSU

Motion slow,
abrupt,
practiced breath,
spontaneous,
routine. . .

like joy.

LEAVES
(by Alice Gates)

Though the trees are bare,
leaves are there.

Steven Swank replies:
The wind is cold,
blowing thoughts of snow.
The night is dark,
the hour is late and though

the tide is out,
it will return, I know.
My harbor heart rejoicing swells
and, finally, lets go.

The promise is the future,
the blessing is today.
We feel the promise turning spring,
marvel in the chapel of love,

the cathedrals of nature,
the immediacy of time.
We hope for a better tomorrow
but live today,

work for the respect of friends,
endeavor, trust.

LIKE WINGS

In evening light
maple tree limbs
ascend in unison.

Stem attachments
on twigs' upper sides
create dynamic lift.

The slightest breeze
causes leafy branches
to uniformly rise

like wings of fledglings
getting set for flight,
flexing in anticipation.

LOST ANGELS

The old man, so blunt,
a fisherman most his life
pulled rhythmically at the oars,
these levers into the sea
so familiar, so elemental;
do they draw, or do they push?

As the early morning fog,
so too his mind
clears by midmorning.
He reckons with patience.
As the last wisps of gray
aspire and finally lift,
he casts his net to starboard
and, here on the water,
finds his peace.

Here too, his heart and soul reside,
though his muscles ache and strength wanes.
More steadfast than strong,
neither careless nor free, he is happy.
Of his weekly routine
this day on the water he favors most.
Will his efforts today be worthy of catch,
the row home worthy of pride?

What do we see across the water?
What do we see in the depths below?
What do we seek when casting nets?

UNFOLD

Where do we go when we row
the heart across a tumultuous sea?

MAN OF ARROWS

He's a man of many arrows
but never shoots at sparrows.

MICHELLE

Your smile pleasantly welcomes conversation,
sharing mutual moments,
endorsing our commonality,
peacefully exchanging well-meaning looks,
joyful recognition of soul, affirming breath.

NO MAPS

Regrettably, some places
do not appear on the map,
important places unfrequented by most.

Among these places:
the narrows between moments,
the breath of the family dog,
drawing lines of the child,
running joy of a kitten,
a morning caucus of jays.

Olive Oil

Living oil for cooks a blessing,
use it in the heating pan
or on salad as a dressing;
other oils it's better than.

Olivine is a volcanic gem.

Open

Pull back the curtain
unlock the window
raise the sash
open the shutters

Unleash the heart
fill the breath
unbind the soul
harbor no fear

Welcome the sunlit breeze
air out the darkened places
attend the drift of caring
expand the sense of self

Turn your back to the clock
notice without judgment
suspend disbelief
let consternation pass

Promote wonder in the mind
inhale peace and hold it tender
exhale the weight of grief
picture your feet in grass.

OPAL

Opal,
Sanskrit: *Upala*, meaning precious stone,
showing translucent colors, sublime.

Cracks, crevices, voids in rock
fill with water-borne silicates over eons of time,
transform into opal vein's translucent colors.

How like opal, without compare,
you shimmer iridescent,
paraselene by day, moon dog at night:

opalescent pearl,
beautiful luminary gem,
an echo deeper than the chime.

OUR SPACE/TIME

*"The interplay between energy and the curvature of
space time has a dynamic consequence."*
—*Sean Corroll*

We for our part as individuals bend reality.
We interact with each other as orbiting bodies,
warping, stretching our mutual time/space.

Paper Stars

Cut out paper stars
put your dreams on a string

hang them brightly above the bed
let them shine overhead

if they tear or fall to floor
get the scissors out once more

begin again with just a few
or cut them quickly in a spew.

Stars will help to lose your sadness
turn the tears to gladness

one of the greatest joys of ours
is to live among the stars.

Politics Perhaps

Perhaps he has eaten
too much angry paste:
You can see it on his face.

Pressure Waves

Pushed by tugs, ocean liners, freights,
pressure waves become the wakes.

Exploding stars also make waves,
warps that rumple space/time.

Shore line depths get redefined,
pulled by the moon in tidal flow.

Turbulent landmass upheavals
fracture buildings, glass.

Storm surge swells to island lee,
pounding surf—then dead calm sea.

Raindrops patter the farming pond;
crosshatching adjacent rings expand.

Early morning rowers on the river
dip oars in silent catch of swirls.

Loons in the moonlight paddle and drift,
call in turn, then take to flight.

Buses and trucks in motion
sway roadside vegetation.

The painter's fingers press
the bristled push of color.

Avian toes in the backyard bath
cause ripples, rebound in mirth.

We in our population math
create waves that pressure earth.

Prompt Spring

Spring is here too soon,
trees obviously confused
by weather so warm.

I miss the bundle and cold,
the challenging path of ice,
snowflakes' buzzing swarm.

Put away toboggan, sled;
put away snowboard, skis:
apparently no more fun.

Delicate snowdrops blossom,
good friends advise me, Smile
and be cheery like the sun.

Longingly, I look for winter,
for the chill, the frostbite,
frozen fingers numb.

Sadly, snow shovel and hat
get stowed in the basement,
where I notice my greening thumb.

STEVEN SWANK

PUPPETEER

Puppeteer, as is his wont,
begins anew each story told
in the mind of the audience,
images warm enough to hold.

The idea here, he says to self,
is to tell a tale in simple lines,
find within the verbal text
a way to linger in their minds.

Let the metaphor grow by nature;
small, particular, noble heart gives,
accumulates novelty, engenders trust,
so they believe the puppet lives.

Slowly at first, they stop seeing us—
we are just the movers, to be fair,
that bring the inanimate to life;
they soon forget that we are there.

QUESTIONS

Some days I ask myself,
what are the questions?

The culturally uncomfortable questions
I fear, I avoid—
questions so problematic
that they seem unmanageable,
unanswerable.

Reflective Light

Midday slack waves roll patiently,
ribbon shimmers of light
lap in conversation—
grace and innocence in child speak,
testing vowels and space.

As I sit reflective at the river
a mallard swims nearby
then joins me on sun-warmed stone,
our relief from the chilling breeze.

He calls to his mate beyond the quay,
when she finally swims near,
he hops down;
they swim out to lunch
on the incoming tide;
the rising water laps at my toes.

They swim together parallel in form
thirty yards offshore, pause to feed
and then, rest floating,
bodies touching side by side.
Perhaps this is how they sleep.

A pigeon lands next to me. Its gossamer neck
reflects the sun, rose, and green.
As I move to avoid the wet,
it steps forward and drinks.

RON

We eat retirement cake,
your photo printed in frosting—
fifty years of percussion
prepares you for a painter's life.

Crows at adjacent tables
peck around the edges,
from the lake nearby
ducks around our feet.

She Stopped

She was so
frightened by the lines,
she stopped coloring.

SNAKE

The snake among shadows
in the shallows of this pond
basks in a spot of sun;
the October air is chill.

I squat to watch its breath so slow,
expand the breadth of tubular lung
and try to match the pythonic rhythm,
reflecting commonality and will—

how different yet the same
in our subcortical need,
each expressing sentience
in our patterned way.

Someday

Hardly grippy, somewhat shy,
I'm just a guy you walked on by.

Perhaps you noticed but did not say;
I hope we meet for real some day.

Speak the Words

Be fair, be just, speak what you must,
unleash the words from your brain,
pry them from their hidey hole,
ascertain the arching theme,
dare to predict, do no harm,
unconfound the past, be plain.

See what you can from afar
but park conveniently nearby,
cry out loud, sound the alarm,
pry the lid off the jar,
work the anvil, hammer, strike
the words while they're hot.

Scrape them from your bare feet
if they be foul or rancor prone,
leave them in the rutty yard
if you can't control them;
unbind, unbend, unintend
the shot from the grassy knoll.

SPRING HOUSE

We bathe in the sunshine,
we bathe in the light,
bathe in the spring house
and stay all night.

Starlight

Among so many you stand out;
your warmth illuminates dark corners,
so even the shadows smile.

Your presence, friend,
brightens the moments we're apart
like the smell of pastries on the tongue.

STONE HEAD

As the truck driver navigates a tight curve
over the mountain pass, rear wheels
abruptly drop off the pavement.

The forty-foot stone head of the governor
being transported to a ceremonial site
breaks loose when the trailer overturns.

Lurching inertia snaps chains,
hurls the head across the road
then plummeting down the palisade.

In tumbling, crushing descent
with all the noise and bluster
of its destructive namesake,

it gouges the landscape,
smashes through trees,
plunges off the cliff face,

in declamatory freefall
hits the water face down
in a terminal splash.

Without comment,
the river flows around it.
Fish swim in the eddy.

Stopping by the Church
on a Fiery Evening

The teenaged girl not yet fourteen
told nine-one-one what she had seen
through the chapel window—
orange and flickering, what did it mean?

I called, she said, so you would know
it's more, I think, than just a glow.
Soon trucks arrived with blaring, lights,
just as flames began to show.

Slickered men with hoses might
save the church, if done right.
But sacredness could not dissuade
the consuming pyre of the night.

In the discerning bright of day
as charred remains get hauled away,
the pastor counsels, Let us pray,
the pastor counsels, Let us pray.

TANGENTIAL REVELATIONS

When we write, it is as a conversation with ourselves. What we read, observe, witness in the sharing, mouthing words in our mind, placing particular phrases, even peculiarness, the associations endeavor to reveal who we are.

TELEVISION BATH

They bathe us in the useless, pathetic,
profane products of plastic and cultural nonsense;
even while lying in the dentist's chair,
the incessant television blares down at me.

Please, I say, turn that off, it offends me.
I would rather listen to the drill,
watch the dentist maneuver his tools
than endure the pain of that drivel.

THE PIANIST CHOOSES

The pianist chooses the piano less flat.
Once we swap it, he'll play on that.

THE WAY OF SALT

Silent, each at our pace
fortify and measure,
find our common place,
what it is we treasure.

At the appointed time to flow
foreign tongues unfold
how differently we are alike
if the truth is told.

From the mine or from the sea
salt is dried in sun;
so the same, you and me,
once we are begun

Internal pressures show,
expose how raw the edges,
how shape begins, unhurried lace,
as tears track down the face.

Tough

You are tough as elm—
woven, fibrous,
unsplittable grain.

Yet there inside
a tenderness still dwells
that quite exceeds your brain.

TROUBLESOME FONTS

He wrote with a great nonchalance
to meet the criterial wants,
endeavored to greet
in metrical feet,
but couldn't decide on the fonts.

TWO VIEWS

You called me Mister Coffee Pants
because I looked at you askance,
and though I much prefer askew,
it isn't something that I do.

The comfort creature, a feline
with countenance to counter mine,
looked out the window in disdain
and saw me soaking in the rain.

I climbed a ladder for her to see
me pantomime the door, a key;
I pleaded that she let me in.
She licked her paws, gave me a grin.

UNIQUE

Older,
many years having passed,
she wonders now,
descending from the bus,
her steps in rain unconcerned,

how she found out
when she'd been so unsure.
Why had she not known
whom she must become,
what the catharsis was
and where it must lead?

She is happy,
heedless of the marks of age,
hopeful each day of rising,
hungry when food is present,
or, lacking that, content.

She walks near dark, near dreams,
past the docks toward town.

VOID

The great void,
the vacuum of which
is constantly pulling
against my back,

I know full well
if I misstep
the abyss is waiting
to swallow my soul.

I do not look back;
moving forward,
I improvise,
find my way.

WALK

Of course I think of you and how
we've walked together from then to now.

WANT, GET

Motionless, the fawn stays hidden,
kite lifts on freshening breeze,
and the poem unfolds unbidden,
children say, "Yes, thank you, please."

Gratitude greets generosity,
as anger meets ferocity;
kindness too engenders trust,
necessity becomes a must.

Our presence makes us smile—
be it goodness or just style,
among forever's multiplicity,
our souls know implicitly.

WHAT A WONDERFUL DISGUISE

You wear the theater
as a wonderful disguise,
arriving early,
leaning back earnestly
in the corner adjacent
to ascending stairs,
the red partition drapes
pulled open.
Your long black dress and heels
reveal a purposeful intent,
though what it is
does not show on your face.

Taking little notice,
well-dressed men and women
begin to fill plush seats with chatter.
Your vision is closed to them,
wrapped in thought, arms folded,
face bathed in light.

STEVEN SWANK

WON'T NEEDN'T

This poem won't wait
    won't waver
        won't regret

This poem needn't worry
    needn't insist
        needn't apologize

How should I reshape
    the poems
        you send?

I choose not to pour them
    into the vessel
        of my bias.

WORRY

The flags snap and chatter,
the sun is up, the wind chill.
As I sit on the yellow curb,
you are in surgery.

They cut and sew what needs doing.
I worry,
distract myself with pastry,
shiver in the sun.

You Who

I incline uphill
toward the precipice
along the edge
in awkward balance
to find you

You, who waken the morning
with early light,
you who underpin
the flight of birds,
cause humble math
to predict the path of stars

You, arranger of lupine and lily
in mountain meadows,
bringer of joy to the table,
knower of anomalies,
definer of terms

Your grace and beauty
unsettle my resolve,
unhinge my tongue,
delineate time,
coalesce dreams.

YOUR FLEDGING

Feathers, tiny feathers,
emerge during sleep—
a fuzz at first,
spreading up from ankles,
almost unnoticeable,
unusual, but not rare,
alarming, but not painful:
The Icarus Syndrome.

Perhaps months pass before you notice
the untreatable condition.

If, some mornings, shoulders ache,
you have been flapping in your sleep.

Around the waist feathers elongate,
become more than down.
The shafts catch under clothing,
expose themselves through sweaters.

Long flight feathers encumber arms,
especially in the shower;
clumsy, they hang lank.
Take them into the sun.

Shiver the arms,
stretch out to dry,
acknowledge them as wings.

You Decide

I am happy you take the chance.
Let this book your life enhance,
read aloud with Joe, amuse,
then for other purposes use—
doorstop, trivet, shim,
these naturally occur to him,
but you decide how is best
to put this book to the test.

INDEX OF TITLES

CPSIA information can be obtained
at www.ICGtesting.com
Printed in the USA
BVOW10s0804090617

486367BV00001B/2/P